The Wisdom of Jacob Böhme

Edited and with an introduction by
Arthur Versluis

Great Works of Christian Spirituality

New Grail

Library of Congress Cataloging-in-Publication Data
Böhme, Jakob, 1575-1624.
   [Selections. English. 2003]
   The wisdom of Jacob Böhme / edited and with an introduction by
   Arthur Versluis.
   73 p. cm.-- (Great works of Christian spirituality ; v. 2)
   Includes bibliographical references and index.
   Contents: On spiritual life--Dialogue with an enlightened soul--On divine
contemplation--On nature--On regeneration--On freedom--How to pray--On
death and the Last Judgement.
   ISBN 0-9650488-6-1 (alk. paper) $6/04$
  1. Mysticism. 2. Theology, Doctrinal. I. Versluis, Arthur, 1959- II. Title. III. Series.

   BV5095.B7 .
   [A25 2003]
   248.2'2--dc21

                                        2002035803

                    New Grail Publishing
                    St. Paul, Minnesota

                    www.grailbooks.org

                    New Grail Publishing
                    P. O. Box 14285
                    St. Paul, Minnesota 55114

The Wisdom of Jacob Böhme

Contents

Volume II in *Great Works of Christian Spirituality*
Series Editor: Arthur Versluis

The Wisdom of Jacob Böhme

Introduction by Arthur Versluis

Jacob Böhme (1575-1624), sometimes in English called "Behmen," is arguably the most influential and profound spiritual author of the modern period. His influence, both in Europe and in North America, is much greater than most people realize. Philosophers, artists, literati from Georg Wilhelm Frederic Hegel to William Blake and Ralph Waldo Emerson, all found inspiration in the extraordinary books and treatises written by the "inspired cobbler." Indeed, he is the origin of a non-sectarian esoteric spiritual tradition called "theosophy," the chief figures of which I have detailed in a number of books, including *Theosophia*, *Wisdom's Children*, and *Wisdom's Book*. Though not well known, this tradition (which has absolutely nothing to do with the nineteenth-century occultist movement of Blavatsky that attempted to take its name) continues to the present day. But more important than Böhme's influence, wide and deep as it may be, is Böhme's profundity. In this little book, we can see for the first time the wisdom of Böhme in lucid contemporary language; here, we find a concise manual for the contemporary spiritual seeker who looks for true depth in the Western spiritual tradition.

Böhme's life is well known, and discussed in detail in numerous other books, so there is little sense in repeating what can be found elsewhere. What is more, this series of books is meant to offer what we may term a manual of spiritual advice, and in this respect is meant to be more practical than academic. Still, it may be of value to outline broadly the arc of Böhme's life, as to do so helps underscore the nature of his work. There are many legends about Böhme's early life: it is said that he was visited by a stranger who predicted his spiritual illuminations in later life; and there are other apocryphal stories about him as well in much the same vein. We know from his own testimony that he had a profound spiritual illumination while in his twenties, and that although he led a fairly ordinary lay life as a man who married, had children, and worked as a shoemaker in Görlitz, Germany, (very near what in the twentieth century was divided by the iron curtain into Poland), he also developed very profound insights into nature and into the spiritual life.

His initial insights he wrote down in order to keep them fresh for his memory, and when the resulting manuscript, under the name *Aurora* began to circulate more widely, it came into the hands of his local Lutheran minister, one Gregorius Richter. Richter was incensed against Böhme's writings, perhaps not least because of Böhme's warnings against what he called "Babel," or the mere outward pretense of Christianity without any inner spiritual awakening. Whatever the reasons, Richter began to persecute Böhme, and for more than a subsequent decade, Böhme obligingly ceased from writing and publishing further books or treatises. But then, later in life, Böhme was prevailed upon by his circle of spiritual friends to write down more of his insights, and it is from this time of late productivity that most of his work dates. During this period, Böhme wrote an astonishing number of very complex spiritual and cosmological works, as well as numerous letters of spiritual advice to seekers. Böhme died in 1624, reportedly with the words "Now I enter into paradise." Although his grave was later defaced by his persecutors, his readership only continued to grow, especially after Johann Georg Gichtel's publication of his complete works early in the eighteenth century.

Böhme's books have a reputation for being extremely complex, even impenetrable, but much of this is due to the cosmological dimensions of his work, and to his often circular, repetitive, and dense style. When he sought to explain his insights into the hidden aspects of nature, he drew upon alchemical language and neologisms that for most modern readers seem totally opaque. While there are glossaries and explanatory works like his *Clavis* or *Key*, these often seem only to intensify the reader's sense that although there is much that is profound in Böhme's work, it remains beyond most of the rest of us. On the other hand, though Böhme's insights (especially those into nature) are indeed difficult, many of these belong to his earlier writing, for his later works include much that is very simple and clear. It is chiefly from these kinds of works that this collection is drawn.

Why is it that Böhme has had such a vast underground influence and sparked so many spiritual pilgrims' inner journeys for centuries? Certainly it is not because of his insights into hidden aspects of nature alone. No, in Böhme's work, spiritual seekers in Europe, England, and North America in particular found an opening into a rich spiritual life. This inner life is not at all concerned with the foundation of yet another sect, and indeed, for this very reason there are no theosophic churches or even any public organization in the Böhmean tradition. The only such sect was that of the English Philadelphians under the leadership of Jane Leade, herself a visionary but not really in the Böhmean current in the way that, for example, the great spiritual author John Pordage (1608-1681) (her contemporary) was. What attracts spiritual seekers to Böhme's works is their realization that here is a profound and humble guide into the treasures of the inner life; here in Christianity is an author whose work is much closer to Sufism in Islam, or Kabbalah in Judaism, but who clearly belongs entirely to the Western spiritual lineage, and who reveals great spiritual mysteries.

In this collection, I have chosen selections from a range of Böhme's works, and have edited and translated them into a lucid contemporary aphoristic form. In this way, it becomes clear that Böhme's advice to the spiritual seeker is both practical and profound, and is based only on his direct personal experience. For this reason, this collection both begins and ends with selections from his letters to various correspondents, in which he refers to his own experiences and spiritual growth. Other books from which these selections are drawn include *Six*

Theosophic Points, *The Way to Christ*, *Three Principles*, and *Forty Questions*. All that is included in this collection was chosen because it offers direct advice to the spiritual seeker on how to enter into and complete the inner journey of spiritual awakening.

Böhme's genius lies, in part, in his ability to convey this spiritual advice in the larger context of his spiritual understanding. While this collection does not emphasize his insights into the hidden aspects of nature, it does include this part of his work because it could not be otherwise—one cannot understand his advice to the spiritual seeker without recognizing that it belongs in the context of his theosophic perspective as a whole. Böhme's work reveals not only the human relationship to the natural world, but also the human relationship to the spiritual realms, most notably, to the various aspects of the divine. According to Böhme, during our brief lives on earth, we have the possibility of spiritual illumination that will have profound ramifications for us in the afterlife. For him, Christianity is not merely "Babel," or outward show and belief in merely historical events, but a process of inward transmutation and illumination.

In this respect, Böhme's visionary insights are very much akin to Buddhism: central to his understanding is the concept of the *Ungrund*. The *Ungrund* literally means the not-ground, and belongs to a long tradition in Christianity of negative theology that begins with Dionysius the Areopagite, and can be traced through Meister Eckhart, Böhme, and his successor, John Pordage, to name only the most stellar exemplars of this current. About the *Ungrund* Böhme writes in his *Dialogue of an Enlightened and Unenlightened Soul* as follows. The disciple asks about the nature of love, and the master replies: "Its virtue is the Nothing, and its energy is in everything. Its height is God and its breadth greater than God. He who finds love, finds the Nothing in the all." The disciple is puzzled, and asks "How am I to understand this?" The master replies:

When I say 'Its virtue is the Nothing,' it means that when you leave all creaturehood, and become a Nothing to all nature,— then you are in God himself, and then you will experience the highest of virtues: love. And when I further say that—'He who finds love finds the Nothing and the All,' it is also true, for he finds a supersensual *Ungrund*, without an abiding place, to which nothing can be compared. One therefore compares it with Nothing because love is deeper than the 'I'. It is a Nothing to all things because it is incomprehensible. Because it is a Nothing, it is free of all things. Love begins all things, love rules all things. If you find it, you will enter the Ground from which all proceeds and in which all exists: then you are lord of God's works.

 The Nothing of which Böhme writes here may well be compared to the Buddhist concept of *shunyata*, often translated as "emptiness." Just as emptiness in Buddhism is said to be identical with compassion, so the Nothing in Böhme's understanding is identical with love.

Böhme is often identified as a visionary, and this is no doubt true, but the term in itself may be misleading. Usually, the term implies visionary encounters with personified divinities, but in Böhme's case, it refers to something rather different. Böhme's vision was much more comprehensive than what is usually understood as "visionary": he offers a complete metaphysics and cosmology. His metaphysical vision extends into what he calls "eternal nature," by which he means divinity as it manifested itself to itself in creation prior to the existence of the physical cosmos. Eternal nature exists in the *Ungrund*, sometimes also termed the "Abyss;" in it are what Pordage calls the "simplified spirits" of God, as well as the angels and paradise. Understanding Böhme's metaphysics is critical to understanding the practical spiritual advice that he offers the reader, for the two cannot be understood separately from one another. Böhme is a visionary, but his visionary insights are into metaphysical reality far beyond what is usually understood by this term.

The heart of Böhme's advice may be understood as contemplative practice, that is, the practice of relinquishing self-will into silence and allowing the divine will to manifest in us. Several times in his work he offers advice along the following lines: "Were it possible for you to remain quiet for an hour in your inner self-will, then the divine may speak through you. Through this inward-speaking, God brings his will within you into him, entering into the natural, outward life of discursive reason, shattering the earthly imagination of the rational will and illuminating it so that the supersensual divine life blooms in the discursive reason." What is more, "As the selfish will is quiet from activity and sinks beyond all nature, so the divine speaking, within the resigned life, appears. For when one enters the silence of self-will and is in the abyss, there God speaks. If self-creation and self-willing cease, divine creativity and divine will emerge." We are called, in Böhme's work, to enter into contemplative silence and to enter the abyss—the *Ungrund*—where divine creativity can manifest itself in us because our sense of a divided self vanishes.

This contemplative practice in turn opens us to inner freedom, the freedom that comes from the disappearance of a sense of separated self and of the selfish will that accompanies it. As a result, Böhme writes, "That which consists in eternal freedom, if it remain in eternal liberty, it has no darkness; it is as free as the eye of God, which beholds itself reflected in being." This inner freedom is, paradoxically, total submission to the divine will. When we are subject to all the conflicting desires and furies of the individual self, when we are buffeted about and misled by the *spiritus mundi* (the spirit of this world) and caught in our own sense of a separated self, we are not free at all, but when we sink down into the resigned life of inner awakening, we are freed from those attractions and aversions and enter into a new way of life; we are regenerated or born anew.

What is the process of regeneration as Böhme outlines it? In our present state, we live in a restless condition, perpetually seeking what we cannot find around us: a state of rest. Our problem is our misguidedness: we seek peace in what is transient, wanting to grasp and hold what is in fact as transient as smoke, the things of this world. All that we seek to

grasp continually disintegrates, so we live in a
condition of suffering. What is the solution? It is
offered us by divine grace: in Christ, Böhme writes,

> God's love breathed into this captive and confused life, re-
> awakening its divine essence so that it could transcend its
> painfulness and restlessness. Since the great love of God in
> Christ thus came within an earthly image to the aid of human
> life, making a divine entrance to grace for poor humanity, our
> enslaved will of life, caught in its earthly imagination, must
> foresake the earthly selfishness and give itself up to this grace.
> Uniting with this grace, it must sink with the resigned life-will
> into the supra-essential freedom of the eternal One, into the
> origin of life itself. It must surrender into the ground from
> which life itself emerged. Here it is again in its eternal rest, in
> the *tempermentum*.

This is the process of regeneration condensed into a
few sentences.

The importance of undergoing this process of
regeneration extends far beyond this individual
mortal life. For if we do not undergo regeneration,
then after death we remain caught in what we were
during life: but our body is gone, and we remain as a
discarnate, restless being seeking in frustration and
anger, which in turn become our own judgement
against us. This Böhme makes clear throughout his
work, for the theme of regeneration is the center of all
that he writes. After death, he pointedly notes, we do
not "go" anywhere, for heaven and hell are principles
that interpenetrate the world in which we live now.
After death, we manifest what we have attained
spiritually in this life; what is already in us, becomes
our condition. If we are full of anger and greed, we

will not be happy after death; if we are regenerated, then we enter into divine life.

Böhme consistently denigrates "Babel"—purely conventional outward Christianity that is based on mere historical belief and the appearance of piety. To "Babel" also belongs all the speculations of discursive reason applied to religious matters, and this includes historical prophecies of "end times." He bluntly remarks that we should ignore questions of historical prophecy like that concerning the "thousand-year Sabbath" or millennium in Revelation, and concern ourselves with our inward life, adding that "We have enough in the Sabbath of the new birth, for the soul that attains this inner Sabbath of regeneration will, after the death of the earthly body, have Sabbath enough in paradise." Speculation about historical prophecy belongs in the end to worldly history and so far as our inner life is concerned, is as fruitless as a hypocritical Christianity full of false piety, bluster and empty rhetoric; what matters is that we awaken spiritually in this life.

This spiritual awakening or regeneration takes place through prayer. Prayer, for Böhme, is not petitionary in the conventional sense. He writes:

Prayer is not an act like that of a man who comes before a worldly king or lord against whom he has transgressed, asking for his grace while thinking differently in his heart. No! An emanation of God, man should surrender himself to God with all his powers, with all that he is, and all that he owns.

Hence:

If you want to pray truly, then turn away from all creatures and
come before God undefiled in will and mind, in determination
and sincerity. Though discursive reason will say 'You will not
be heard; your sins are too great,' or 'Now is not the time; wait
and first do this or that so later you will have leisure,' do not be
mistaken. God's vitality acts in the inner ground, in the will's
yearning. Just be silent and wait for the Lord. Your yearning
will eventually penetrate so you will feel it in your heart and
thank God.

Prayer is the practice through which the process of
regeneration originates and takes place; it is an
inward contemplative journey, not merely a series of
verbal requests, but an inward process of
illumination.

From all of this, we begin to see that Böhme is in fact
revealing a comprehensive esoteric Christianity, a
way of understanding nature, divine life, the world,
ourselves, and the process through which we come to
spiritual understanding. These selections, though for
the most part they are simply written, clear, and
aphoristic, are very profound, and are not meant to be
scanned once and then forgotten. Rather, they
represent a series of insights into the nature of
spiritual life, and are meant to be read and reread,
held in the mind, contemplated. They each exist with
a certain space around them, and the more one works
with them, the more profound they reveal themselves
to be. This is a brief book, to be sure, but don't let its
brevity lead you to conclude that it is a slight one. For
here you will find the most profound of Christian
authors, one whose work opens up whole new ways

of understanding. This book may well be characterized as the heart of Böhme's work, made as lucid as his work has perhaps ever been. May it be as much a treasure for you as it is for me.

Vale.

Select Bibliography

Jacob Böhme, *Samtliche Schriften*, (Stuttgart: Fromanns, 1957)

____, *The Epistles of Jacob Böhme*, (Glasgow: Thomson, 1886)

____, *Forty Questions*, John Sparrow, trs., (London: Watkins, 1911)

____, *Six Theosophic Points*, (Ann Arbor: U of M Press, 1958)

____, *The Way to Christ*, John Stoudt, trs., (New York: Harper, 1947)

____, *The Way to Christ*, Peter Erb, trs., (New York: Paulist, 1978)

____, *Three Principles of the Divine Essence*, (London: Fowler, 1909)

Serge Hutin, *Les Disciples anglais de Jacob Boehme aux XVIIe et XVIIIe siècles*. (Paris: Editions Denoël, 1960)

Nils Thune, *The Behmenists and the Philadelphians: A Contribution to the Study of English Mysticism in the 17th and 18th Centuries*. (Uppsala: Almquist and Wiksells, 1948)

Arthur Versluis, *Theosophia: Hidden Dimensions of Christianity*, (Hudson: Lindisfarne, 1994)

____, *Wisdom's Children: A Christian Esoteric Tradition*, (Albany: SUNY, 1999)

____, *Wisdom's Book: The Sophia Anthology*, (St. Paul: Paragon House, 2000)

The Wisdom of Jacob Böhme

On Spiritual Life

The whole Christian religion consists in this: that we learn to know ourselves, what we are, where we have come from, how we left unity and entered into multiplicity, evil, and disjointed, strife-filled life, and where we are to return from this life in time. All that is necessary for us to know about religion derives from this: to come out of disunity and vanity, and to enter again into the one tree from which all of us stem: which is Christ in us. Everyone who seeks to teach outside of God's spirit and has no divine understanding, yet wants to serve God by teaching, is a false guide.

My dear friend, I will not conceal from you the simple, childlike way that I walk in Christ Jesus, for I can write nothing of myself, but am like a child that neither knows nor understands anything. For I never desired to know anything of the divine mystery, much less understood the way to seek or find it; I knew nothing of it, as is the condition of poor laymen in their simplicity. I sought only the heart of Jesus Christ, that I might hide myself therein from the wrathful anger of God and the violent assaults of the devil. I asked the Lord for his Holy Spirit and grace, that he would be pleased to bless and to guide me.

In this earnest seeking, during which I endured many trials, until I was at last resolved to lay my life on the line than to give up, and then the gate was opened to me, so that in a quarter of an hour I saw and knew more than if I had been many years at a university. For I saw and knew the being of all beings, the Byss or ground of all things, and the Abyss, the Ungrund, bottomless and fathomless. I saw the birth of the Trinity, the original of this world, and the origin of all creatures, through the divine Wisdom. I saw in myself the divine, angelic, paradisal realm; the dark world; and then the external visible world, which appeared as a substance manifested from the inner or spiritual worlds. I saw and knew the essence that works in good and evil, and how the pregnant mother (genetrix, or fruitful bearing womb of eternity, brought forth. At all this I was full of wonder and rejoiced.

Eventually I decided to set this down in writing, as a mnemonic device for myself, even though I could hardly understand it in my external man or express it with my pen. I had then begun to labor in these great mysteries, like a child that goes to school: I saw (as in a great deep) into the inner realm, for I had a full view of the cosmos within a chaos, wherein all things are wrapped up, but it was impossible for me to explain this.

Yet it opened itself in me from time to time, rather like a young plant that grows, and this happened for twelve years, and I was as it were pregnant with it, and found a powerful impetus within me before I could bring it forth into an external form in writing. Afterward, it fell upon me like a sudden shower, that hits whatever it falls upon. Just so, whatever I could apprehend and bring into the external mind, that I wrote down.

The sun shone on me a good while, but not in a constant manner, for when it hid itself, I scarce knew or understood my own writings. Man must acknowledge that his knowledge is not his own, or from himself, but God's and from God; and that God manifests his wisdom in the soul of man according to his own measure.

Thus I have written not from knowledge received from men, nor from the learning or reading of books, but out of my own book opened within me, the noble similitude of God, the book of the noble and precious image was bestowed upon me to read. In it I have studied, like a child in the house of its mother, who beholds what the father does and in his child-like play imitates his father. I have no need of any other book.

My book has only three leaves, the three principles of eternity, wherein I can find all that Moses and the prophets, Christ and his apostles have taught and spoken. I can find therein the foundation of the world and all mysteries, yet not I, but the spirit of God does it according to his own pleasure.

No man must think more of me than he sees, for my studying and writing is none of mine; I have it only according to the measure the Lord is pleased to give me. I am nothing but his instrument, whereby he effects what he wills. This I related to you, beloved friends, lest anyone esteem me other than I am, as if I were a man of high art and deep understanding and reason, for I live in weakness and infirmity in the childhood and simplicity of Chirst.

But because, dear friend, I see you are seeking in this way, I write you, and offer you this answer: self-reason (being void of God's spirit) taunts, derides, and despises whoever does not conform to the canons and institutions of the universities and high schools, which I do not wonder at, for this self-reason is from without, and God's spirit is from within. This self-reason is like the wind, which is driven to and fro; it esteems human judgement, and those self-reasoners who have the respect of the world do judge and censure. But it doesn't know the mind of the Lord because that mind is not in it; its understanding is from the stars, and only a counterfeit shadow in comparison with the divine wisdom.

Whereas the children of God have diverse gifts in writing, speaking, and discernment, they do not have only one manner of expression. Hence self-reason by artifical conclusions draws out of them what it wishes for itself, and creates a Babel, whence such a wearisome heap of opinions arises. Thus out of their writings men have invented diverse conjectures, and others are forced to go in those ways. Out of this comes controversies and unchristian contentions, making many disputes about the outward letter, but this is nothing but Babel, mother of spiritual whoredom. Reason doesn't enter into the door of Christ through Christ's spirit, but seeks to climb by its own might and pride, being unregenerated, and always wishes to be the fairest child in the house so that men honor and adore it.

The Father's wisdom is immeasurable, and through his wisdom all things arise. So the souls of men are constellated in great diversity, but they originally proceed out of one essence. The spirit of Christ opens the property of every soul, so that each speaks from its own property of the wonders in the wisdom of God.

I have no controversy with the children of God by reason of the diversity of their gifts. I can reconcile them all in myself: I just bring them to the center, and there I have the touchstone of all things. If you will imitate me, perhaps you will find it so by experience and better understand what I have written.

Doesn't a bee gather honey out of many flowers? And though one flower is better than another, she doesn't hesitate to take what serves her. If the sap of the flower is not good enough, does she sting it as the despiser and mocker does? Men argue much about the shell of knowledge and religion, but pay no attention to the precious sap of love that serves life.

God is in heaven, and heaven is in man; and if man desires to be in heaven, then heaven must be manifest and revealed in him. This must be brought to pass by earnest repentance and unfeigned self-denial, and this we may do as well at home in our own places. That which you think to run from, you are like to run into.

I never in my life studied these mysteries, and knew nothing of them, for I am only a layman, yet I find I must bring such things to light that all the universities have not been able to do, to whose understanding I am in comparison only a child, without any of their art or wisdom. I write wholly from another school, for the language of nature is known to me, so I can understand the greatest of mysteries in my mother's tongue.

Though I cannot say that I have comprehended it, as long as God's hand is upon me, I understand it; but if his hand hides itself, then I do not understand my own labor, and am a stranger to the work of my own hands. By this I see how impossible it is to apprehend the mysteries of God without God's spirit. I ascribe nothing to myself; it is not my work, and I seek no human applause for it. I am only a simple, mean instrument. What God wills, I will also.

Though I must leave my outward body and life to the world to do as it may, and though the devil roars against me, still I will trust neither the devil nor the world with my inner man, nor will I do what the world would have me do. Though my outward man is bound to the world and its laws, so that I do what the outward obligations require, yet my inner man is only obedient to God, and not the world. For the inner man is not in the world but dead to it, that God might live in him.

In my work there is an open gate of the mysteries of all beings, and there is nothing in nature that might not be discovered in this way, for it opens the stone of the wise men, revealing all secrets and mysteries in the divine and earthly mysteries. By this knowledge, all the metals of the earth may be brought to the highest degree of perfection, yet only by the children of the divine *magia*, who have its revelation.

No one can see the being of God externally; the spirit sees God in itself, and in its own fellow-creatures, for God is the spirit of all beings. So when we see the divine creature, then we see an image proceeding from God's being, and in the will of that creature, we see the will of God. Thus is the new man born of God, for we know nothing of God without God's spirit. The external cannot see the internal, but if the inner draws the outer by a glimpse into itself, then the outward apprehends the mirror of the inner, and sees that the outer takes its origin in the inner, and that our works shall follow us into the mystery and that by the separation of God's judgement in the fire of the principle, they shall emerge in the eternal world.

The outer world is of God, and from God. Man is created in the outward world that he might bring the outer figures into the inner, that he might bring the end into the beginning.

I see well enough, but I only set forth an open mystery, wherein God will find laborers of his own. Let no man seek the work from me, or try to get the philosopher's stone from me, though it is known clearly in my work.

I pray that God will open to you the door of his love in the mystery, and crown you with the diadem of his wisdom, which is more precious than the created heaven and this world, for the precious philosopher's stone, the ground of all mysteries and secrets, lies therein. This diadem of wisdom is inset with this philosopher's stone, which the soul puts on as a garment, a new body in and for the kingdom of God. In this new body it can stand in the fire of God's anger without any harm, and can rule over the stars, the baleful influences of the constellation, and this outward life, which is impossible for reason alone. This crown gives the knowledge of things that external reason cannot penetrate; it sees into heaven and earth, and reaps where it has not sown, and asks not the question: is it true or not? It has the sign of truth in itself; it has all virtues in hope, it is not afraid of God's anger.

This garland is a virgin and divine beauty; through it the mind rejoices in affliction. It goes with us into death, but has no death in it; it lives from eternity and is a guide into heaven; it is the joy of the angels. Its taste is more precious than all the joys of this world, and he who obtains it, esteems it higher than all the riches of this world. It is of the deity, but it lies hid in a dark valley. The world doesn't know it, and the devil blows against it. But it springs forth in its own time as a fair lily with manifold fruits. It is sown in tears, grows in tribulation, and reaped in joy. It is condemned and despised by reason, but he who obtains it realizes it is his greatest treasure.

Dialogue with an Enlightened Soul

The disciple said to his master: "how may I come to the supersensual life so that I can see and hear God?" The master replied: "When you can enter even for a moment into that where no creature dwells, then you can hear God."

Disciple: "Is it near or far?" Master: "It is within you. Could you cease will and thought for one hour, then you could hear God's inexpressible word."

Disciple: "How can I hear when I stop will and thought?" Master: "When you stop willing and thinking, then transcendent hearing, seeing, and speaking is revealed within you, and God will see and hear through you. Your selfish hearing, willing, and seeing hinders you from seeing and hearing God."

Disciple: "With what shall I hear and see God, since God is beyond nature and creature?" Master: "When you are silent, then you are as God was before nature and creature came into being. Then you are like that out of which he created your existence in nature. Then you will see and hear by the same means by which God 'saw' and 'heard' within you before your selfish willing, seeing, and hearing began."

Disciple: "What prevents me from achieving this?"
Master: "Your selfish willing, hearing, and seeing prevents you. You are hindered by your own striving against that out of which you came. The self-centeredness of earthly material life closes off your hearing, leading you into a ground, and overshadowing you with that which you will so that you can't come into the supernatural, supersensual life."

Disciple: "To do this, must I forsake the world and my life?" Master: "Insofar as you forsake the world, you will come into that out of which the world was made. Insofar as you lose your life and realize your own impotence, will you be in him for whose sake you lost it, in God out of whose body you came."

Disciple: "God created man in the natural life to rule over all the earth's creatures and to be lord of life in the world. Therefore man must own the world as his property." Master: "If you rule outwardly over creatures, then you are bestial in your willing and ruling, living only in a transitory realm. Worse, if you let your desire enter into bestial essence, then you will be infected by it, and acquire animal form. But if you forsake images, then you are beyond the world of images, ruling in that ground beyond all beings out of which they emerged. Then nothing on earth can harm you, for you are like all things, and nothing is unlike you."

Disciple: "O master, teach me how I may come to be like all things." Master: "If you want to be like all things, then you must forsake all things and turn your desire away from them. Nor must you seek to acquire and possess a 'something.' For when you include the 'something' in your desire, and accept it as a possession, then the something enters into you and becomes a part of your will. But if you appropriate Nothing into your desire, then you are free of all things and at the same time rule over all things. Through your acquisition, you have nothing, and are a nothing to all things, and all things are nothing to you. You are like a child, not understanding what things are, and even though you do understand, your understanding is without self-consciousness, in the same way that God rules over all things and sees all things without being comprehended by any being. How do you come to this? Christ said: 'without me you can do nothing' (John 5:5). By your own ability, you can't attain this rest wherein nothing disturbs you. But when you surrender yourself fully into the life of Jesus Christ, wholly giving up your will and desire to him, then you are at the beginning from which all creatures emerge and to which they again return. Then you may contemplate outward things with your reason, inward things with you spirit, and with Christ, to whom all powers in heaven and earth are given, you are able to rule over all things" (Matt. 28:28).

Disciple: "O Master! These creatures living within me prevent me from yielding myself, no matter how much I want to." Master: "Christ said: 'If you abide in my words, then my words abide in you.' This means that if your will enters into creatures, then you have broken away from him, and you can be rescued in no other way than by remaining in humility and by repentance, so that you are grieved that these creatures live within you. When you do this, then daily you are dying to creatures and ascending into heaven with your will."

Disciple: "How can I be free of temptation?" Master: "If every hour but once you can leap out of all creatures, beyond all sensual thought, into the pure mercy of God and the suffering of our Lord Jesus Christ, surrendering yourself to it, then you will receive the power to rule over sin, death, the devil and the world. Then you will be firm against temptation."

Disciple: "What would happen to me were I to reach with my mind into that place where no creature dwells?" Master: "O dear disciple, if your will could break away from all creatures for only one hour, it would be in the majesty of divine glory. Then it could taste within itself the sweetest love of Jesus Christ, which no man can describe. Then it could experience within itself the inexpressible words of the mercy of Christ. Then it would feel that the cross of Jesus Christ had been changed within itself into tender joy, and that it would rather win this than all the world's honor and wealth."

Disciple: "Since the body must live among creatures, what becomes of it?" Master: "The body will follow our Lord Jesus Christ, who said: 'My kingdom is not of this world.' Outwardly, it will die to the world's vanity; inwardly, it will die to all evil inclinations. It will develop a new mind and will that are always directed to God."

Disciple: "But it is hard to be despised by the world!" Master: "That which now seems heavy, you will later learn to love the most."

Disciple: "Dear Master, why must love and suffering, friend and foe, live together? Wouldn't it be better if love stood alone?" Master: "Without suffering, there would be nothing to love or to release from pain. Love could not be known were there nothing to love."

Disciple: "What is love's virtue, energy, height, and breadth?" Master: "Its virtue is the Nothing, and its energy is in everything. Its height is God and its breadth greater than God. He who finds love, finds the Nothing in the all."

Disciple: "How am I to understand this?" Master: "When I say 'Its virtue is the Nothing,' it means that when you leave all creaturehood, and become a Nothing to all nature,—then you are in God himself, and then you will experience the highest of virtues: love. And when I further say that—'He who finds love finds the Nothing and the All,' it is also true, for he finds a supersensual *Ungrund*, without an abiding place, to which nothing can be compared. One therefore compares it with Nothing because love is deeper than the 'I'. It is a Nothing to all things because it is incomprehensible. Because it is a Nothing, it is free of all things. Love begins all things, love rules all things. If you find it, you will enter the Ground from which all proceeds and in which all exists: then you are lord of God's works.

Disciple: "Where does love dwell in man?" Disciple: "Love dwells in that place within oneself where one is not."

Disciple: "How may I attain love without dying to my self-will?" Master: "If you want to attain it for yourself, it will shun you. But if you yield yourself fully to it, then you are dead to your self-will and then love will become the life of your bestial nature. Love doesn't kill you; it enlivens you. Then you live, yet not you, but love's will becomes your will. Then you are dead, yet live in God."

Disciple: "Why do so few people find love, since so many gladly would have it?" Master: "They all seek it in selfish desire, as an imagined meaning, to which all have a natural, selfish inclination. Although love offers itself to them, it can find no place within them, for their imaginative selfishness wants to own it. Thus love flees, for it lives only in the Nothing, and there the selfish will cannot find it."

Disciple: "No longer can I stand being wrong. What is the nearest way to love?" Master: "Walk where it is hardest to walk; accept what the world rejects; shun what the world does. In all things go against the world and you will come to love by the nearest way."

Disciple: "Where does the soul, be it good or evil, go when the body dies?" Master: "The soul doesn't go anywhere. The outward, mortal life and the body separate themselves from it. All along heaven and earth were within it. So it is written: 'The kingdom comes not with outward signs: neither shall they say'"Lo, here!" or "Lo, there!" for behold, the Kingdom of God is within you' (Luke 17: 20-21). Whichever of these two states, hell or heaven, become manifest in the soul, in that state it stands."

Disciple: "Doesn't the soul go into heaven or hell just as a man goes into a house or as one passes through a passage into another world?" Master: "No. There is no such entering. Heaven and hell are present everywhere. There is only the transmutation of the will into God's wrath, or into his love, which actually takes place in corporeal life."

Disciple: "How does this entering of the will into heaven or hell take place?" Master: "When the will gives itself up into the divine ground, then it sinks beyond itself, beyond all grounds and conditions, into the only place where God is revealed, where he works and wills. Then it becomes a Nothing to its own selfish will. Then God works and wills within it.

When the body dies, then the soul is permeated with divine love, and with divine light, just as a fire reddens iron. This is the hand of Christ. When God's love is wholly infused into the soul and it becomes a shining light and a new life, then it is in heaven; it is a temple of the Holy Spirit. But the godless soul doesn't want to give up its will in this life to divine self-forgetting. Instead, it follows its selfish inclinations, and goes about in vanity and error, in the devil's will. It appropriates only evil, falsehood, arrogance, greed, envy, and wrath. To these it resigns its will, and its vanity becomes manifest in it. So when the body separates from the soul, then eternal lamentation and doubt begin, for it finds it has become an anxious, useless abomination, and is ashamed to try to enter into God with its false will. Indeed, it is caught by wrath; it is become wrath. It has locked itself up in wrath and awakened wrath in itself. Since God's light does not shine in it, it is in deep darkness, a painful, anxious fire-source. Wherever it is, there is hell! Even if it could throw itself hundreds of thousands of miles from itself, still it would be in such a condition of darkness."

Disciple: "How is it that the holy soul cannot perfectly experience that great light and joy in this life? How is it that the godless soul cannot feel hell, since both are in man?" Master: "Within holy souls, the kingdom of heaven is experienced through faith. They feels God's love in that faith by which they have given up their wills to God. The holy soul often is full of anxiety when hell presses in on it. But it inures itself in the hope of divine grace and stands like a rose among thorns until the world falls away from it at bodily death. Then, when nothing hinders it, it becomes manifest in God's love. In the meantime, it walks with Christ in this world. Christ will deliver it from its own hell and stand with it in hell, changing hell into heaven. Why do the godless not feel hell in this life? I answer: they do feel hell in their own consciences, but they do not understand, for they are still caught in their own earthly vanity. The external life still has the light of outward nature, in which the soul takes pleasure and it doesn't feel the inner pain. But when the body dies, it finds itself in eternal hunger and thirst for its vanities, but it can attain nothing but a false, self-centered will. Because in this life it had too much and was not content, now, when it has too little, it hungers after wickedness and frivolity. It would gladly do more evil, but there is no way to complete it, so the completion is only in itself. But this hellish hunger and thirst cannot become wholly manifest in you until the body dies."

Disciple: "Since heaven and hell thus are at war in this world, and since God is so near to us, where do the angels and devils live?" Master: "Where you with your selfish will do not live, there the angels live in you. Where you live with your selfish will, there the devils live within and without you."

Disciple: "How far are heaven and hell from one another?" Master: "Heaven is throughout the whole world, and beyond this world it is everywhere without division or place. It exists in itself through the divine manifestation. And where it enters or where it becomes manifest, there God is revealed. For heaven is a manifestation of the eternal one in which all works and wills in love. Similarly, hell is through the entire world, operating only in itself and in that where hell's foundation becomes manifest as egotism and false will. The visible world contains both heaven and hell. Man in time is only in the visible world, and during life does not see the spiritual world. But when man's body dies, then the soul's spiritual world becomes manifest, either according to the eternal light with the holy angels, or according to the eternal darkness with the devils."

Disciple: "What is an angel, and what is man's soul, that they can realize God's love or wrath?" Master: "They have a common origin. They come out of the eternal ground from which light and darkness arise. Just as darkness lies in egotistic desire, so light lies in willing with God. When the soul wills with God, God's love works; in the egotistic will, God's will also works, but painfully, producing darkness that light becomes known. Both are manifestations of divine will, in light or in darkness, according to the properties of the spiritual world."

Disciple: "What will happen after this world with all its things that pass away?" Master: "Only physical substance ceases to be: the four elements, the sun, moon, and stars. The inner spiritual realm will become completely visible. But whatever man has done during his time in this world, be it evil or good, each such act shall separate itself into eternal light or eternal darkness. That which a will has conceived will press back in upon it in a state corresponding to its nature. Darkness will be called hell, as an eternal forgetting of the good; and light will be called the kingdom of God, eternal joy and endless praise of the saints now released from pain. The last judgement is the kindling of the fire of divine love and wrath. In it all physical nature will perish, and will take on the fire according to its nature. All born to God's love, everything that draws the love-fire of God into itself, will give itself up to that love-fire. But all that exists in the darkness of divine wrath will draw painfulness to itself and consume this false substance, and then the selfish will remains in its own pain."

Disciple: "In what form or matter will our bodies be resurrected?" Master: "The human body is a natural, rough, elemental body that correponds to the physical world. But within this rough body there is a subtle vitality, just as there is a subtle vitality in the earth that is akin to and even one with the sun, and that originated in the divine vitality. This good vitality of the mortal body will appear again to live in a beautiful, transparent, crystalline matter. Likewise, the good vitality of the earth will become crystalline, illuminated by divine light. Just as the crude earth will disintegrate and not be restored, so too man's crude flesh will perish and not live eternally. In the judgement, all will be separated by fire, both the earth and the ashes of the human body. In the spiritual world then, each spirit will assume its substance, the good spirit assuming a good substance, an evil one an evil substance. By 'substance' you should understand a kind of vitality, for 'substance' is energy, like a tincture. What is crude or gross will perish."

Disciple: "But will we not then rise in our material bodies and live in them forever?" Master: "When the visible realm disintegrates, then all that is external also perishes. The world continues in a heavenly, crystalline aspect. Only spiritual earth remains in man, for then man is become like the now hidden spiritual realm."

Disciple: "Will there be man and woman in the spiritual life? Children and family? Will they associate with one another as in this life?" Master: "How fleshly-minded you are! There will be neither man nor woman, but all like the angels, male virgins, not daughter, son, brother, or sister, but one race in Christ, like a tree with its branches, separate creatures, but God all in all. Then there will be spiritual knowledge of what each has been and has done; there will be no possessiveness, and not even the desire to possess."

Disciple: "Will they be equally blessed with eternal joy and glorification?" Master: "Paul writes: 'in the resurrection they will differ from one another like the sun, moon, and stars' [I Cor. 15:41]. All will enjoy divine providence, but vitality and illumination will differ. It will be with an individual according to the degree of his anguish. In this time, anguish generates divine vitality by which God's power works. Those who have worked with Christ during this time and who have not given in to fleshly passion will have great vitality there and a wonderful glorifcation. But others who have served their belly-god, only to be converted in the end and attain grace, these will not receive so great a vitality. There will be a differentiation as between sun, moon, and stars, or like among the flowers in the field, with their variety of beauty, vitality, and virtue."

Disciple: "Where will the devil and the damned be cast, since then the whole world will be glorified as Christ's kingdom? Will they be driven to a place beyond this world, or will Christ manifest his dominion beyond this world's sphere?" Master: "Hell will remain in this world to the end but it shall be hidden in the heavenly kingdom, just as night is hidden in day. Light will shine eternally in the darkness, but the darkness cannot comprehend it. Light is Christ's kingdom, the darkness is hell, where the devil and the godless live. They will be suppressed by Christ's kingdom and become in reproach, a footstool."

Disciple: "How will it go on judgement day with those who torment the poor, oppressing them, forcing them, trampling on them as footstools, just so they themselves may vaunt themselves vainly?" Master: "All such people do this to Christ himself, and they will meet his stern judgement. For they oppress

Christ, persecute him, help the devil, and draw the poor away from Christ, so that they seek easy ways to fill their bellies. They do what the devil himself does, in continually resisting Christ's love-kingdom. All who do not turn their whole heart to Christ and serve him must enter into hell's fire where vain selfishness belongs."

Disciple: "Why does God allow such strife in this time?" Master: "Life is full of strife in order that it may become manifest and so that wisdom may be known. Strife serves the joy of victory. For in Christ's saints there will arise great jubilation that Christ has overcome the darkness and selfishness of their natures within them, and released them from strife. God allows everything to exist with free will so that the eternal dominions of love and wrath, light and darkness, may become manifest and known, and so that each life may awaken its own judgement in itself. That which is to the godless a worldly pleasure will be changed into eternal pain and shame. The joy of the saints arises in death just as the candle's light arises in the dying flame, so that nature becomes free of pain and possesses another world. Just as light has a different property than fire, giving itself by consuming itself; so also the holy, humble life blooms in the death of the selfish nature, and then God's love-will rules in all things. For this the eternal One took on sensibility, and by sensibility brought himself forth through death into the mighty kingdom of joy, so that there would be eternal play in the endless unity, and an eternal cause of the kingdom of joy. Painfulness must give rise in its ground and origin to motion. And in this there lies hidden the *Mysterium* of God's Wisdom. 'Ask and it shall be given you, seek and you shall find, knock, and it shall be opened to you' [Matt. 7.7]. The grace of our Lord Jesus Christ, the love of God, and the Communion of the Holy Spirit be with us all. Amen.

On Divine Contemplation

Reason says: I hear many say that there is a God who has created all things, who sustains them, but I have not met anyone who has seen this God or who could tell me where or how he is. When I look at the world's nature and consider that it goes as well with the impious as with the pious, that all things are transient, and that the pious find no redeemer to free them from the anguish of evil, then I think that there is no God who cares about those who suffer, and no one has ever been heard of who returned from corruption and been with God.

Answer: Reason belongs to nature whose basis is a temporal beginning and ending, and it cannot attain the supersensual ground wherein God may be understood. Yet Reason does experience in itself a longing for the higher ground wherein it may find peace. For at heart, Reason knows that it originated from a supersensual ground and that there has to be a God that brought it into living and willing. It is frightened by its willing of evil; it is ashamed of its own selfishness. It fears an unseen judgement, which signifies that the hidden God brought himself into nature and lives within it. Reason seeks rest in something other than itself. It wants its ego to die, but does not want to be a nothing. Instead, it wants to die to anguish and find rest in itself. Here one begins to understand how the hidden God manifests himself in man's mind, awakening his conscience, and how rational life through suffering achieves a longing to turn itself back again into that out of which it came. Reason must want to hate itself and die to its natural will so that it may attain a supersensual will.

Reason says: Why has God created a painful, anguished life? Since he is the ground and beginning of all, would it not have been better without anguish? Why does he tolerate evil? Why doesn't he destroy evil so that only good remains?

Answer: Without duality, nothing can become manifest to itself. If there is nothing to resist it, then it constantly emerges out of itself but doesn't return back into itself. And if it doesn't return to itself, into that from which it originated, then it knows nothing of its original state. If natural life had no dialectic, and was without limit, then it could never seek the ground from which it came. The hidden God would remain unknown to it. Had the hidden God, who is one essence and will, not brought himself out of himself, how would the hidden will of God become manifest to itself? How could there be self-knowledge in an undivided will?

Reason asks: What is good or useful about the presence of evil with good?

Answer: Evil activates the good to seek its own essential state again, to press in upon God, making the good desirous of good. What is good in itself, wants nothing, seeks nothing, since it knows nothing better within itself or for itself to which it might be drawn.

Reason says: Since mind is a created, natural life, in a particular time, how may it attain the supernatural divine life? What is the divine indwelling in life?

Answer: Human life is a mode of the divine will; it is the imagined *Logos* of divine knowledge, but has become poisoned by the devil's breath and by the wrath in temporal nature. Because of this, humanity stands in an earthly image, which may be understood in terms of three principles. The first principle exists in the emanating will of God, in divine knowledge, a real paradise or realization of divine powers. But when this life in the first principle was tinged by the wrathful devil, it was persuaded to break off from this life and enter into its own image, to experience evil and good. When the knowledge of individualities became manifest, nature established its rule, life became painful, and the inner divine ground became extinguished. Life's will broke away from life and entered into multiplicity. Thus the second principle, the divine kingdom, was extinguished, and the third principle, the source of the stars and the four elements, the gross body, and the earthly senses, emerged.

Life lost its eternal rest and by its desire made itself dark, painful, hard; life became restlessness, and lives in the realm of earthly power, seeking rest in transience, where it can find no rest. Life vaunts itself above the stars and elements, and has become mad in its dominion. It cannot know its own origin in earthly creatures or in selfishness; foolishly, it has left the divine and entered the beastly, wanting to dominate and grasp that which is as transient as smoke. What it seeks to grasp perpetually disintegrates, so life remains opposed to the first principle, and so is merely an eternal becoming, an inextinguishable fire-source, as the devils and demons are.

But God's love breathed into this captive and confused life, re-awakening its divine essence so that it could transcend its painfulness and restlessness. Since the great love of God in Christ thus came within an earthly image to the aid of human life, making a divine entrance to grace for poor humanity, our enslaved will of life, caught in its earthly imagination, must foresake the earthly selfishness and give itself up to this grace. Uniting with this grace, it must sink with the resigned life-will into the supra-essential freedom of the eternal One, into the origin of life itself. It must surrender into the ground from which life itself emerged. Here it is again in its eternal rest, in the *tempermentum*.

Reason asks: But how can we do this, since the Bible says that man is to have dominion over all creatures?

Answer: Christ said [John 15:5] that without me you can do nothing. By your own power, no one can achieve the highest ground, except by sinking your innermost ground of the first principle and become silent in your own being. In divine hope yielding yourself wholly to God's will, so much that your own will no longer seeks after that ground— yielding to what God speaks and wills through that ground— you attain the highest goal.

Were it possible for you to remain quiet for an hour in your inner self-will, then the divine may speak through you. Through this inward-speaking, God brings his will within you into him, entering into the natural, outward life of discursive reason, shattering the earthly imagination of the rational will and illuminating it so that the supersensual divine life blooms in the discursive reason.

As the selfish will is quiet from activity and sinks beyond all nature, so the divine speaking, within the resigned life, appears. For when one enters the silence of self-will and is in the abyss, there God speaks. If self-creation and self-willing cease, divine creativity and divine will emerge.

That which is without will is one with the Nothing and is beyond all nature, for *Ungrund* is God himself. The *Ungrund* is an exhalation of God himself, and so is spoken into the resigned life. The inner, regenerated life, in divine vitality, shall dominate the external life of discursive reason, which belongs to the realm of stars and elements. Indeed, if the inner life does not dominate the outward, earthly, astral life of temporal inclinations, and break the earthly will in which the serpent-monster lies, then there is no new birth. So long as you are in the earthly will, you are not a child of heaven. For this reason, Christ said [Matthew 12:30] that he who gathers not with me, scatters. That is, if you do not will and act with the incarnate grace of God, which God through Christ has offered, but instead work only with the natural selfish will, you scatter your works over a false ground.

Consider the sun as a parable. If an herb has no sap, it is burned up by the sun's rays. But if it has sap, then the sun's rays warm it, and it grows. So also is human life. If it has none of God's meekness and love, then it becomes a violent fiery sharpness, so the mind becomes raw, devouring, greedy, envious, bristling, and such a temperament scatters all that is good. All that it touches is poisoned. But if this fiery life eats of the divine love, it ceases being greedy, and becomes generous. For the love-will gives itself, like light from a fire, radiating good toward all things.

If the soul breaks off from resignation in the *Ungrund*, it becomes sharp, fiery, dark, raw, envious, antagonistic, generating restlessness in itself, and leading itself into a transient, doomed, fierce wrath. This is its damnation. Yet if such a fire-source attains divine love and comprehends divine light in itself, it will be transmuted into a kingdom of joy. But this is only possible for a redirected will.

On Nature

In the beginning was the *Logos*, and the *Logos* was with God, and the *Logos* was God [John 1:1-3].

The beginning of all existence is the *Logos*, the exhalation of God. The *Logos* is the emanation of the divine will and knowledge. This emanation proceeds from God, and what is emanated is Wisdom, the origin of all powers, colors, virtues, and characteristics. In the revelation of these powers, the eternal One beholds itself, for the eternal will contemplates itself in creation, and in Wisdom projects itself into existence. This self-projection of itself to itself is the Great Mystery; here is the creator of all existence, for in it is the Separator of the will's emanation, which makes the divine will differentiated. In this differentiation of will, all powers and characteristics arise.

Yearning is the origin of the individual will, for in it the separated wills come into self-consciousness, by which is to be understood the true, angelic, soul-life.

The divine will is in itself not comprehensible, and is free of any bias or yearning, for there is nothing toward which it might incline except itself. Thus it leads itself out of itself, emanating its unity into plurality, and into the assumption of self-existence, that is, into a natural state in which individualities arise.

Thus the Separator of each will brings qualities out of itself, from which the infinite plurality emerges, and by which the eternal One makes itself manifest through its emanation. In this way, eternity brings itself forth into nature through characteristics and individual life, manifesting the visible realm.

God's essence therefore is not a differentiated thing, with any particular abode, for the abyss of nature is God himself.

The visible world and all its creatures is nothing but the emanated *Logos* manifested in individualities, within which self-wills emerged. There are thus two modes of life: an eternal, and a temporal.

The innermost ground of a being is a spark of the will of God, emanated through God's exhalation. This spark, emanating from the *Logos*, wills only that which God's will wants in such an emanation.

The spiritual world of fire, light, and darkness is hidden within the visible, elemental world. This spiritual world acts through the visible world, and imprints itself through the Separator upon all things, to each according to its individuality. The outward is merely an instrument of the inner spirit.

In all growing things, we see three kinds of spirits in distinct centers, yet in one body. The first is the gross sulphur, salt, and mercury, which is the substance of the four elements or the stars, and which makes the body. The second is the oil of sulphur, known as the quintessence, the root of the four elements and of the first spirit. This receives its nutriment from the light of nature, from the inner spiritual fire and light, but also from the sun and subtle vitality of the *spiritus mundi*. This is the essence of growing life, the joy of nature, like the sun itself. The third spirit is the tincture, also known as paradise or divine delight. From it all vitality arises, for the tincture is a spiritual fire and light. It is the highest ground out of which the differentiation of individualities arise, and it originates from the holy vitality of God. From this high and holy origin flows the vitality of all in this world.

This revelation we see in all living things.

When I see a plant, I truthfully say: this is an image of the spirit of the earth in which all the higher powers rejoice, and which they regard as their child. For the spirit of the earth is one with the higher powers. When the plant matures, it blooms, and the oil of sulphur manifests itself in beautiful colors. And in the delightful scent of the blossom, the tincture, or third principle, manifests itself.

In this we see that the inner hidden spirit of the elements manifests itself and forms fruit. The earth would not have such scents or colors if the hidden vitality of the divine emanation did not reveal itself.

So it is also with the metals, which outwardly have a gross body of sulphur, mercury, and salt, but inwardly they are a transparent, beautiful body, within which shines the light of nature from the divine emanation itself. In this light we see the tincture and how the hidden vitality makes itself manifest.

This I can truthfully say of all that I see, evil or good: here in this thing the Separator of all substances has manifested itself into individuality, representing itself according to its emanatory nature, be it evil or good. All manifests according to the individualities of nature, heat and cold, bitter, sweet, sour, or however it may be. In all such manifestation there is an elemental aspect, but in the inner ground, in its tincture, it is good and beneficial, part of the nutriment of life.

Everything, be it plant, grass, tree, animal, bird, fish, worm, or whatever else, is beneficial, and has emanated from the Separator, that is, from the *Logos*, or differentiating will of God.

For this visible world is nothing other than an image of the spiritual world hidden within the material realm just as tincture is hidden in herbs and metals. Just as the tincture makes itself visible in all things through colors and scent, so that humanity can know the nature of the Separator or emanation of divine will, so too one can see in the visible world, in sun, stars, elements, creatures, in all creation, that inner ground out of which they emerged.

Elements are nothing other than the imaged, moving substance of the invisible and unmoving.

The stars themselves are an emanation of the individualities of the spiritual world, whose essence is the *Logos*, or differentiating will of God.

Every hard matter, such as metals, stones, wood, herbs, and the like, has in it a noble tincture and high spirit of life-force, just as do bones, for the noblest tincture of vitality is in the marrow.

Everything in this world that is soft, gentle, and etheric is emanating and self-giving, and its origin is the unity of eternity, for this unity is eternally emanating from itself.

Thus is it to be understood of the noble tincture: where it is noblest, there it is the most hard. For in it the unity is contained in movement. In what is etheric, it is not perceptible, but it is the same in all things, just as water and air are in all things.

But the true Pearl-ground is found in dry water, in which the subtle life-power of the movement of the unity in the *centro* is contained. To those of us who are worthy of this, know we should not appropriate

to ourselves the soft apart from the fiery nature,
seeking the mystery therein. Understand the mystery
this way: the soft and etheric emanated from the unity
out of the great mystery, and is the nearest to the
unity. By contrast, the noblest ground of the divine
revelation lives in the life-power of the fiery hardness,
a dry unity in which is contained the differentiation of
all life-forces. Where the life-forces are not borne
within the unity of a will, the will is divided, and
there is no great life-force in what is divided. This
should be carefully studied by physicians, for they
should not look to the coarse spirit or sharp scent and
regard it as the true balsalm, even though the tincture
within it is quite volatile. Enclose all of these life-
forces in one, so that they have one will in love, and
then you have the Pearl of the whole world.

But provoke the life-forces to wrath creates pride and
strife, which can be seen in all things.

One can only comfort a prisoner with freedom. The
prisoner must will hopefully, composing himself in
patience, until his restlessness finally becomes hope,
enters the *tempermentum*, and he learns humility.
Then he rejoices when one informs him of his release.

You physicians, consider this well: this is your Pearl,
if you would but understand it. The meaning of this
is both inward and outward.

On Regeneration

In John 1:11-13, we find this: Jesus Christ came into his own, and his own received him not. But those who received him, to them he gave power to become children of God, who were born, not of blood, nor of the will of the flesh, or of man, but of God. The ground of divine manifestation lies in these words. For they speak of how the hidden, divine, eternal *Logos*, the divine life-force in unity, proceeded out into the manifested, natural, imaged realm, i.e., into human nature. The manifested *Logos* is the property of the eternal *Logos*—hence "his own." But the misdirected, selfish will did not receive him, because it wants to be its own Lord. But that will which has turned about, so that it has been newborn in the divine, he has given power to be a child of God. The natural, selfish will cannot inherit divine childhood, but only that which is joined to the unity, is one with all things, and in which God himself wills.

Man is not at home in this world, but is come into it as a guest, and has not brought the clothes of this world with him, but must borrow strange clothing from the children of the stars and elements. With this strange clothing, he struts and preens, supposing he is very fine in it, yet it is but borrowed from the spirit of this world, which in due time takes it away again.

The holy element in nature continually longs to be released from the vanity of the four elements. The spirit of this world longs that man should seek the great wonders that are in it, and bring them to light. Through man, the noble tincture may be brought to light, so that paradise might appear, and so that nature might be freed from vanity.

We poor humans have left our native country, the incorruptible, and entered a strange inn, where we are not at home but are merely guests who may be thrown out at any time. We find ourselves in a deep sea of misery, and it is most necessary for us to find our way back to our true native country, that we may avoid this great misery and reënter our eternal inn.

But because there are these two inns, the one in eternal joy, brightness, and perfection, love and meekness; and the other in anguish, misery, hunger, and thirst, so it is necessary that we learn the way of entrance into the eternal joy.

Now if we look about us among the stars and elements, we see no way to rest; we see only the end of our life, when our body goes into the earth, and another inherits all our labor (including our arts and glory), vexes himself with it, and then follows after us. We can in our misery not know where our spirit abides when our body becomes a carcass, except if we are newborn out of this world, so that we dwell in this world in our body, and in our mind in another eternal perfect new life. Then we know what we are, and where our home is.

The writings of those who have been regenerated out of this earthliness and entered into a holy and incorruptible life, they teach us how we should follow them and enter into a new birth, a new creature. In this very life, we can see our true native country through our own regeneration, and know it in great joy.

There is in this new birth the greatest and highest love, not only toward God and oneself, but also toward our brothers and sisters. Those who have been regenerated, so love humanity that they teach with meekness and reproof, and their love for humanity is so great that they even yield their body up to death.

We also have longed after that pearl, and though now the unregenerated in the world will give no credit to us, we cannot help that, and it shall stand for a witness against them, a woe to them in eternity, that they lost so great an eternal glory and holiness for a little pleasure of the eye.

And there is no remedy for the unregenerate, save regeneration through the heart and light of God, through which the new element is regenerated (the body of the soul.

The Virgin, the Wisdom of God, is the spirit of this pure element, and is therefore called a Virgin because she is so chaste or pure and generates nothing, but rather like the flaming spirit in the human body, opens all great wonders in the holy element. Here are the essences, wherein the fruits of paradise spring up. As this pure element (the presence of God) is truly everywhere in the space of this world, and has attracted to it the kingdom of this world as a body, and yet this body does not comprehend this element, so too Christ has put on our human being and become our brother, yet human beings cannot comprehend his eternal deity. Only the *homo novus*, the new man, comprehends the deity.

As Adam opened the gate of wrath, so the deity of Christ opened the gate of eternal life so that all men can press in to God through this opened gate. For the third principle [nature] is broken here.

In this world there are fire, air, water, and earth, as well as the sun and stars. Likewise, you may think of the Father as the Fire of the constellations, and the Son (his heart) is the Sun; and the Holy Ghost is the air. The *spiritus majoris mundi* [the spirit of the great world] is the chaste Virgin before God. For the deity is incomprehensible, and invisible, yet perceptible; but the Virgin is visible as pure spirit, and the one holy element is her body, which is called the holy earth. Into this holy Ternary the invisible deity is entered, that she may be in eternal union. Deity is in the pure element, and the element is the deity. This is the heavenly Virgin, and this holy ternary is our true body in the image that we lost.

O blind wolves of Babel, what have we to do with you? We are not from your kingdom. Is it a sin for us to inquire after our true native country? Can the kingdom of God be found in your scorn and vexation? Where is your apostolical heart, full of love? To you it is said: the wrath burns in Babel; when the flame rises up, then will the elements shake and tremble, and Babel will be burned in the fire.

The temptation of Christ shows us his person, so open your eyes, and don't let Babel trouble you.

Beloved reader, I will tell you this more plainly yet, for everyone doesn't have the Pearl to apprehend the Virgin. Your soul has all three principles in it: the wrathful source, according to which it is a spirit; the divine virtue, which makes this spirit bright and joyful, so the spirit is an angel, like God the Father; and then it has the principle of the world. Yet none of these three principles comprehends the other, for they are in fact three births. The spirit is eternal, and the other two principles are given to it, one to the right, the other to the left. It is possible for the spirit to lose both births that are given to it, for if it reaches back into the Fire and becomes false to the Virgin, then the door to the Virgin is shut. But if you turn to the Virgin again, you must be born anew through the water in the center, through the Holy Ghost, and then you will receive her again, with much honor and joy.

About this Christ said: "there will be more joy in heaven for one sinner who repents than for ninety-nine righteous who need no repentance." This joy none can express, for only a regenerate soul knows it.

These two principles or births, the spirit loses at the departure of the body, and that which was an angel now becomes a horrible fierce poisonous worm. If the worm had had no angelic and human form, then its torment would not have been so great, but that causes it to have an anxious desire, and yet it can attain nothing; it knows the shadow of the glory it had, and cannot live in it again.

This in brief is what can be said about the fall of Adam and the new birth. Adam has lost the Virgin by his lust, and the Virgin waits continually for him to see if he will step again into the new birth, for then she will receive him in great glory.

Consider this well: I write here what I know, and he that has also seen it is my witness.

On Freedom

If the sun were taken away from this world, all things would be in darkness, and then outward reason would say "we are in dark death and the wrath of the cold," and so it would be. Consider: when your body perishes, and your spirit loses the sun, how can you enjoy the light?

That which consists in eternal freedom, if it remain in eternal liberty, it has no darkness; it is as free as the eye of God, which beholds itself reflected in being.

When you imagine after anything, in desire, then the will enters into that thing, so that it dwells in darkness until it goes forth again into liberty. Thus we have no light at all in our being and doing, if we let our will enter into our works and covet them. Then we are blind and without light except that of the sun, and when the body dies, the soul is imprisoned by what it desires.

The prison of the soul is a dark cave, and though it inflames itself, it becomes only a wrathful fire-flash, and cannot reach the divine light by itself.

God's eye is thus in two parts: one looks forward into the still eternity, into the eternal Nothing—into liberty. And the other looks backward into desire, creating darkness and the center of nature, with it anguish. But if the will sinks through the darkness into the still freedom, this liberty turns into a triumphant light that shines forever in eternal freedom and desires nothing.

Even if God were to receive your spirit into his majestic light, if you remain in earthliness and desire, you would not be able to experience that light, but would remain in darkness.

Your soul has in it two eyes: the left, filled with longing, and the right, that turned toward the liberty. Let your hands labor, and let the eye see wonders, but don't let them in, for that which is drawn in will be darkness. Let the devil roar at you, making a noise before your left eye, but he cannot get in unless you let him. When your earthly body perishes, you will see with your right eye what you have wrought, and your left eye will be free from wrath. For if your eye has taken into itself nothing of matter, it will be free, and you will then see before God with both eyes eternally.

This is one gate. One who sees and knows this rightly in the spirit, sees all that God is, through heaven, hell and earth, and the whole of Scripture, indeed, all that has been written since the beginning of the world. But this is a rare and precious sight: the old Adam doesn't know it—only one who is newborn in God may know this.

Let me make this plainer. You are in the world and have an honest calling? Continue in it, work, do what necessity requires. Let your art be what it will, for it is all the work of God. But do not let your spirit enter into and fill itself with outward images and darkness, so your noble image is corrupted by your imagination and you lose God's image.

For God's image in you is magical, it is subtle as a spirit, it dwells in eternal liberty, unapprehended by anything. It consists in heavenly flesh and blood in the divine body, and the Holy Ghost sits in the heart of the image, manifesting in languages, wonders, sounds, and songs.

Set your left will on the work that you are called to do, and remembering you are God's servant in the vineyard, labor faithfully. Direct your right will to God, and to the eternal, and do not think yourself ever secure. You are only at your daylabor, and always listen for the voice of your Master calling you home. Give reason no chance to say: "This is *my* treasure; it is mine; I will gather more, that I may have honor in the world and leave much to my children." Recall that your children are God's children, and you God's servant; all your money and goods and mind are his. When he calls you home to your own country, he may take your labor and give it to another.

Give your heart no room to let your will give rise to pride, but remain humble, so your inner image is continually enlightened by the triumphant light of

God. How cheerful is the soul when its anguish-fire tastes God's light!

No one may say of anything in this world: this is mine; I am lord of this. All is God's. Your friend's joy in heaven is your joy, his wonders your wonders.

For in heaven God is all in all; the Holy Spirit is the life in all; there is joy only, no sorrow. All things are common; one rejoices at the power, brightness, and beauty of another; there is no malice or envy, for all that remains in death and hell.

You elect children of God, born again in Christ, depart from desire and self-will; you have been long since led blindly in Babel: go out from her, that you may obtain eternal joy in God.

Thus the soul and the inner image in the spirit are all three one, for they are one essence, like the Holy Trinity. Beloved friend, the soul cannot be enlightened in any way other than this.

How to Pray

Real prayer is not merely repeating words, for mere words without heart-felt devotion and longing for the divine is just an outward act. In the mere repetition of words there is no vitality. God is pleased only by that which he himself works within us.

If we would really pray, we must look first at ourselves, and consider whether our heart has imagined itself into another creature, whether what we want from God is right, or contrary to the love of our neighbor, whether we seek temporal things, whether we bear universal love and singleness of heart, or whether we are only self-aggrandizing.

We should consider what we want, whether we are seeking mere worldly honor, or whether we are a faithful servant in the vineyard. We should recall that in this world we own nothing, we ourselves are not our own, and that we are only guests here, servants here for but a short time.

We should recall that by our own strength, we cannot truly pray. We must depart from all arrogance, falsehood, wrath, envy, and stubbornness. We must yield our whole heart to God, the Holy Spirit, so that he is our strength in prayer.

Prayer is not an act like that of a man who comes before a worldly king or lord against whom he has transgressed, asking for his grace while thinking differently in his heart. No! An emanation of God, man should surrender himself to God with all his powers, with all that he is, and all that he owns.

If you want to pray truly, then turn away from all creatures and come before God undefiled in will and mind, in determination and sincerity. Though discursive reason will say "You will not be heard; your sins are too great," or "Now is not the time; wait and first do this or that so later you will have leisure," do not be mistaken. God's vitality acts in the inner ground, in the will's yearning. Just be silent and wait for the Lord. Your yearning will eventually penetrate so you will feel it in your heart and thank God.

If you want to pray properly, you must forgive all your enemies and include them in your prayers, petitioning God to convert them, to reconcile them to him in his love.

God helps a pure, unadorned, naked soul in prayer. Though the heart forgets or doubts, despite all hindrances, still the will should stand fast and hold grace in it, not wanting to foresake it. Then you will see and experience great wonders in yourself, and you will know it is true that there is great joy and heaven over the repentant soul, more than over the ninety-nine just ones who need no such repentance.

He who prays truly, is with God inwardly, and outwardly bears good fruit. Just as the tree man ifests its vitality in fruit, so the divine vitality in man is seen outwardly in good works. Otherwise prayer is mere hypocrisy, just an outward show.

When the will truly longs for grace, when the will truly begins to leave itself and enter into divine mercy, the divine life-force awakens within it, and then the soul really speaks with God and God with the soul. The soul is nourished by the inner speaking of God, just as a plant is nourished by the sun's vitality, becoming fragrant, growing and blooming. So also the soul is filled with light and vitalized by the divine sun, when it has wholly surrendered itself to God.

If this is to come to pass, the will must leave all creatures and earthly things behind and stand naked before God. True prayer is an embrace of what the soul yearns for, and so Christ said: The kingdom of heaven suffers violence, and the violent take it by force [Matthew 11:12].

Many words are unnecessary: a single sigh suffices with God if the will is naked before him and the earthly cloak has been tossed aside.

On Death and the Last Judgement

I have no knowledge of the thousand years' Sabbath; I cannot ground it well in Scripture, for one place disagrees with another. Men interpret Scripture as they are inclined to do, but seeing that I have no command from God concerning this, I let it and like matters alone, and leave everyone to answer for his own opinion.

But as to the last judgement, there is no need for further searching: it is clear enough what the mystery of body and soul is, and in what condition separated souls are in, with in terms of the last judgement and their lives and differences. The fact is, the manifestation of the thousand years' Sabbath and other questions concerning historical prophecy is not of much importance to the world, especially seeing that we do not have sufficient ground on this. We have enough in the Sabbath of the new birth, for the soul that attains this inner Sabbath of regeneration will, after the death of the earthly body, have Sabbath enough in paradise. We should leave questions like that of the thousand years' Sabbath and prophecy to the divine omnipotence, and wait on God to see what he will do with us when we are in him and he in us.

Everyone shall be with his own works in the mystery, and be judged according to those works. Our works in this world have been wrought in good and evil, and will be separated in the fire of God.

If we would speak of paradise, let alone apprehend it, then we must have clear eyes to see it, for the inner paradisal world and the external world are within one another; we have only left the inner for the outer, and so work in two worlds.

Death cannot separate our works; the fire of God must do it. Everyone in the resurrection will come forth in his own mystery, see his works before him, and feel them in him.

The resurrected will not answer with words, for the kingdom of God is in power, and though the lost shall cry out, still everyone's work will be summoned in power, either rejoicing or tormenting them.

The old body of this world is the mystery of this world, but the new body is the mystery of the divine light world, in the soul is the mystery of God the Father, and the earth with its elements also has mysteries, which will be revealed through the principle of the Father. Then the doors of the mysteries will be opened.

Happy are those who shall have the body of Christ in the mystery of the wrath, for they shall have the soul's fire or the principle of the Father surrounded by the light world, and will feel no pain or hurt and shall pass through the fire. All earthliness or falsehood shall remain in the fire, but the works will be renovated in the fire, freed from their earthly source. The earthly mystery remains in the fire as its food out of which the light arises, and the righteous lose nothing. The works of love brought forth in the new body pass through with the spirit of the soul and remain in the divine image in the source of the light.

The works of love that are manifested in the new body pass with the spirit of the soul through the fire, and remain in the divine image in the lightsource, but the works of the third principle [this world] remain in the firesource.

But that which has been wrought in a malicious way in this world, and has not been repaired through repentance and reconciliation, that falls into the center of nature, the root of the dark world. Evil works will not remain in the fire, for they are swallowed into the dark center, where the devils dwell, and there also goes the evildoer's soul's fire. This soulfire has no matter to make it burn brightly, so it will be a dark, painful source-fire, an anguish that would like to be fiery. This is God's wrath, a dying source.

The principle of the Father, wherein the true soul lives, is a flaming fire that gives light, the image of God, for that light is filled with love, delightful, a cause of nature and of life.

The more you long after God, the more you run after him, the more you come out of the end into the beginning. For the twig of the tree thirsts after the sap of the tree; it desires the tree and draws its sap and influence into it, so it grows to be a great branch. Thus the earnest longing in the human mystery draws the kingdom of God into itself, of which Christ said: *The kingdom of heaven suffers violence, and the violent take it by force.*

The poor captive soul is a hungry magical fire that seeks to attract to itself the divine disclosed essence, and so it feeds on God's being, takes it into itself, and from this spiritual eating, it gives forth a body of light. Thus the poor soul becomes clothed with a body of light, like a candle-flame, and in this body of light it finds rest. But in the darkness of the world, it finds only anguish and trouble.

If the soul had let the body of light be its only master, and not imagined into this external kingdom of this world, then the wrath of God would not have been perceived. The wrath is only perceived in the absence of light and love.

But if the soul leaves all this pride, coveting, envy, anger, and falsehood aside, and does not long after it, then the divine light begins to shine in it, and it obtains an inner eye through which it becomes humble. It wills nothing, desires nothing, but resignes itself into the lap of its mother. It doesn't esteem subtle reason or much knowledge, and though it knows much, it is not conceited, but leaves all the

knowing, willing, and working, wholly to its
mother's spirit.

The devil in the power of God's wrath continually
opposes this precious sprout or twig of the soul,
springing forth from the Tree of Life within us.

With this twig or image of God within us, we are in
Christ without this world, in the angelical world, of
which the old Adam has no understanding, just as the
rough stone knows not the gold within it.

You must unite the end with the beginning, for the
outer world is generated out of the inner. The
wonders of this world belong to the beginning and
were known from eternity in the wisdom of God, not
in the realm of being, but in the mirror of the virginal
wisdom of God out of which eternal nature always
arises from eternity.

To this end, the poor soul stands in the prison of the
astral and elemental kingdom, that it might be a
laborer and reunite the wonders of outer nature with
the light world, and bring them into the beginning.
Even though the soul may be bruised and endure
much, still it is the servant in God's vineyard and
prepares the precious wine drunk in the kingdom of
God.

When we attain the new man in Christ, when we are
regenerated, then we are *already* in the Sabbath, and
only wait for the redemption of the wicked earthly

life. Where do we keep the Sabbath? Not in this world, but in the angelical lightworld.

God is not a God of evil, who desires revenge or torment; the wicked torment themselves, and God has no hand in it.

The old man of the stars and earthly elements must abide in its own region, in this vale of misery, until death, and then all passes into its own mystery till the judgement of God. Then God enkindles the mystery, and everything is separated into its own property. Each world will take in its own harvest, be it good or evil; all shall part as light or darkness.

This revelation is spiritual, and deep in mystery. It requires an illuminated understanding that enters into the mystery of God, and cannot be penetrated by a merely historical consciousness. In no other manner than through illumination can this be understood; it is the mystery of God, and he who can sink into that, he will find whatever he searches for.

I seek only that you come to know the guide of the inner world, and that of the outer world, so that you may be free from mere conjecture and opinion, for in these there is no perfection. The spirit must be capable of the mystery, and God's spirit must be its guide, or it only sees into the external realm of the stars. You should look to your inner guide, see if he seeks God's or his own honor, whether he resigns himself to the cross and only seeks the good of his neighbor. Are you brought into the heavenly school, on the way of truth, to love and righteousness?

For more, you should read my books. Do but read them right, and you will find what the mystery is, the nature of the *byss* and *abyss*, what the being of beings is. Don't be consumed by needless speculation; for he who finds and knows the great mystery, he finds all things therein: God, Christ, and eternity with all wonders are within; the Holy Spirit is the key to it. If you are in the new birth, there is no need for the hard labor of speculation. Seek only Christ in the manger, in the dark stable. When you find him, you will find that he sits indeed at the right hand of God.

There are great mysteries, and deep spiritual numbers, but the wise man hides them, and keeps the tincture secret, for the world is not worthy of them.

For this reason the prophets, and Christ himself, speak in parables, and even to this day, all who enter into the mysteries do not speak otherwise. I tell you this sincerely and in good faith and love, not out of contempt, but from my knowledge and gifts, seeing you desire it of me. I have given you a short hint, what you are to do herein, and entreat you to look upon it in a brotherly way, and with that I commend you to the love of Jesus Christ.

Index